HOW DO WE LIVE TOGETHER?
RABBITS

BY KATIE MARSICO

CHERRY
LAKE
Publishing

Published in the United States of America by Cherry Lake Publishing
Ann Arbor, Michigan
www.cherrylakepublishing.com

Content Adviser: Stephen S. Ditchkoff, PhD, Associate Professor, School of Forestry and
Wildlife Sciences, Auburn University
Reading Adviser: Cecilia Minden-Cupp, PhD, Literacy Consultant

Photo Credits: Cover and page 1, ©Joanne Stemberger, used under license from Shutterstock,
Inc.; page 5, ©Irina B, used under license from Shutterstock, Inc.; page 7, ©iStockphoto.com/
Flutter_97321, page 9, ©Herbert Kratky, used under license from Shutterstock, Inc.; page 11,
©Nick Biemans, used under license from Shutterstock, Inc.; page 13, ©iStockphoto.com/
Tempau; page 15, ©iStockphoto.com/lucentius; page 17, ©MARK DUFFY/Alamy; page 19,
©Gay Bumgarner/Alamy; page 21, ©robertsenk, used under license from Shutterstock, Inc.

LIBRARY OF CONGRESS CATALOGING-IN-PUBLICATION DATA
Marsico, Katie, 1980–
  How do we live together? Rabbits / by Katie Marsico.
     p. cm.—(Community connections.)
  Includes bibliographical references and index.
  ISBN-13: 978-1-60279-622-5
  ISBN-10: 1-60279-622-X
  1. Leporidae—Juvenile literature. 2. Urban animals—Juvenile literature.
  3. Rabbits—Juvenile literature. I. Title.
  QL737.L32M376 2010
  599.32—dc22   2009021478

Cherry Lake Publishing would like to acknowledge the
work of The Partnership for 21st Century Skills. Please
visit www.21stcenturyskills.org for more information.

Printed in the United States of America
Corporate Graphics Inc.
January 2010
CLSP06

CONTENTS

WHO ATE THOSE VEGETABLES?

You cannot believe your eyes. Who ate all the lettuce in your garden? Chances are good that it was a rabbit!

Many people think of rabbits as harmless. Not everyone agrees, though.

You have probably seen a rabbit in your backyard.

Rabbits often dig through soil and eat plants. This makes them pests to farmers and gardeners.

Maybe you think rabbits are cute. You might think they are pests. Either way, we have to share the outdoors with rabbits. We need to figure out how to get along. Are you ready to learn more about rabbits?

Some people have pet rabbits.

LOOK!

Take a close look around your garden. What other animals spend time there besides rabbits? Hint: Birds and squirrels might be there.

7

A CLOSER LOOK AT RABBITS

You know that most rabbits have long ears and fluffy tails. These long ears make it easy for them to hear very quiet sounds.

Have you watched rabbits hop? They move quickly by hopping from one spot to another.

Rabbits have strong legs.

Did you know that rabbits are **mammals**? They are found on nearly every **continent** on Earth. Different kinds of rabbits live everywhere from icy mountains to hot deserts.

Some rabbits live in **warrens**. Warrens are made up of underground **dens** and tunnels.

Have you ever seen rabbits coming out of a hole?

Have you ever seen a rabbit dive into a hole? Can you guess why? Did you guess that they were hiding from other animals? You are right. Dogs and hawks often attack rabbits.

11

Rabbits only eat plants. They chew on grasses and **shoots** in spring and summer. They feed on bark and twigs during fall and winter.

Rabbits need these plants to survive. People do not want their gardens destroyed, though. What are some things we can do to get along with rabbits?

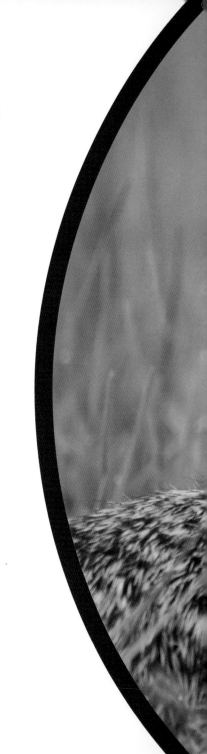

Rabbits eat many kinds of plants.

13

SHARING OUTDOOR SPACES

Rabbits damage gardens. Some gardeners become upset. They trap and kill rabbits.

Other people realize that rabbits are wild animals. Rabbits need homes and food. These people look for ways to live with rabbits.

Traps are not a very nice way to get rid of rabbits.

One solution is to put fences around gardens. This keeps rabbits from hopping in.

Another is to grow onions or **lavender** on the outside of a garden. Rabbits do not like these plants. They might stay away if they smell or taste them.

Does this fence look like it will keep rabbits out?

Other people raise plants that rabbits do like. They grow clover or strawberries far away from their gardens or fields. The rabbits will probably choose to eat these plants instead. This keeps them out of places humans do not want to them to go.

Clover is a favorite food for many rabbits.

Rabbits are just one of many animals that must share outdoor spaces with us. It is our job to find ways to live with rabbits. Then we can all enjoy spending time together outdoors.

It can be fun to watch rabbits that share our outdoor spaces.

Do you want more ideas about how to keep rabbits out of your garden? Ask someone at a gardening store! Gardening experts can help you grow an amazing garden without hurting rabbits.

21

GLOSSARY

continent (KON-tuh-nuhnt) one of seven large landmasses that are found on Earth

dens (DENZ) homes for wild animals

lavender (LAV-uhn-dur) a plant that has pale purple flowers

mammals (MAM-uhlz) warm-blooded animals that are usually covered in hair, have a backbone, give birth to live young, and make milk to feed their babies

shoots (SHOOTS) the first buds of a young plant

warrens (WOR-uhnz) a group of connected dens and tunnels where rabbits spend much of their time

FIND OUT MORE

BOOKS

Endres, Hollie J. *Rabbits*. Minneapolis: Bellwether Media, 2008.

Royston, Angela, and Barrie Watts (photographer). *Bunny*.
New York: DK, 2007.

WEB SITES

The Humane Society of the United States—Rabbits
www.hsus.org/wildlife/a_closer_look_at_wildlife/rabbits.html
Find out more about how rabbits live in the wild.

National Geographic—Animals: Cottontail Rabbit
*animals.nationalgeographic.com/animals/mammals/
cottontail-rabbit.html*
Read about cottontail rabbits, one of the most common wild rabbits
in North America.

INDEX

24

ABOUT THE AUTHOR

Katie Marsico is the author of more than 50 children's books and lives in Elmhurst, Illinois, with her husband and three children. She dedicates this book to her family's rabbit, Waffle.